# TOTALLY AMAZING DAD JOKES

*From Down Under Dads*

**Heta Dawson**
**Corin Healy**

HETA DAWSON  CORIN HEALY

ISBN: 978-0-473-55227-5

TOTALLY AMAZING DAD JOKES

# TABLE OF CONTENTS

Introduction ........................................................................9

Instructions ......................................................................11

Classic Dad Jokes.............................................................12

Knock, Knock Jokes .........................................................65

Dad One-Liners ................................................................86

Punny Dad Jokes ............................................................136

Down Under Dad Jokes .................................................147

Conclusion......................................................................156

HETA DAWSON   CORIN HEALY

# TOTALLY AMAZING DAD JOKES

## © COPYRIGHT 2020 KONNECTD KIDS
## ALL RIGHTS RESERVED.

The content contained within this book may not be reproduced, duplicated or transmitted without direct written permission from the author or the publisher.

Under no circumstances will any blame or legal responsibility be held against the publisher, or author, for any damages, reparation, or monetary loss due to the information contained within this book. Either directly or indirectly.

**Legal Notice:**

This book is copyright protected. This book is only for personal use. You cannot amend, distribute, sell, use, quote or paraphrase any part, or the content within this book, without the consent of the author or publisher.

**Disclaimer Notice:**

Please note the information contained within this document is for educational and entertainment purposes only. All effort has been executed to present accurate, up to date, and reliable, complete information. No warranties of any kind are declared or implied. Readers acknowledge that the author is not engaging in the rendering of legal, financial, medical or professional advice. The content within this book has been derived from various sources. Please consult a licensed professional before attempting any techniques outlined in this book.

By reading this document, the reader agrees that under no circumstances is the author responsible for any losses, direct or indirect, which are incurred as a result of the use of the information contained within this document, including, but not limited to, — errors, omissions, or inaccuracies.

ISBN: 978-0-473-55227-5

**HETA DAWSON   CORIN HEALY**

KONNECTD KIDS
c/- Supply Mechanix LLC
30 N Gould St STE R
Sheridan, Wyoming, 82801
United States of America

www.konnectdkids.com
www.konnectdsupply.com
beawesome@konnectdkids.com
Facebook.com/konnectdkids
Instagram.com/konnectdkids


Illustrations: Marco Angelo Aspera
Edited by Andy Sowden

TOTALLY AMAZING DAD JOKES

## **SPECIAL BONUS!**

Get FREE Books!

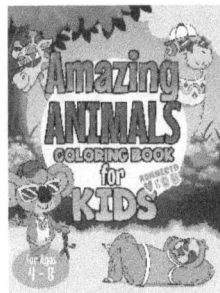  

Konnectd Kids creates Joke Books, Colouring Books, Activity books and many more. Hundreds of others are already enjoying insider access to current and future books, 100% free!

If you want insider access all you have to do is **scan the code below or put the link into your web browser** to claim your offer and join the Konnectd Kids Tribe!

https://tinyurl.com/y5rqbqjm

HETA DAWSON   CORIN HEALY

TOTALLY AMAZING DAD JOKES

# Introduction

A Father sits down with his son who has become a Dad for the first time. "Son, now that you are a Dad, its time I pass this across to you" He hands across a copy of the *Totally Amazing Dad Jokes* book. "Wow Dad, I'm Honored"! "Hi Honored, I'm Dad"

The Dad joke is like a universal language that is understood the world over. It doesn't matter which country you come from every kid has had the experience of growing up with their Dad telling a Joke, or an attempt at one at the very least.

This passing down of Dad jokes from one generation to the next either verbally or in written form is a time honored tradition. Some of these jokes are hilarious, but most of the time they are what is called in the Dad joke world as 'groan worthy!'

New Zealand Comedians Heta Dawson (RAW Comedy Finalist 2019) and Corin Healy (TV Show 'Last Dad Standing' contestant) have compiled and created a total of over 800 jokes including a selection of Down Under Jokes.

## HETA DAWSON  CORIN HEALY

Being Dad's themselves, Corin and Heta have had years of experience in delivering good, bad and terrible Dad jokes to their kids, kids friends, comedy club audiences and anyone else who would listen.

The *"Totally Amazing Dad Jokes"* book from Down Under Dads, has the best Classic Jokes, Knock Knock, Punny Jokes, One Liners, and funny laugh out loud or roll your eyes and groan Dad jokes around.

We hope you enjoy this book and use it wisely as the power of a lifetime of Dad jokes is now in your hands.

TOTALLY AMAZING DAD JOKES

# Instructions

How you want to use this book of Dad Jokes is up to you. You can read them to your family or take turns reading them out.

A good laugh is best shared, so one suggestion is that you can take turns with different players asking the questions and other family members giving their best shot at answering them.

Whatever way you decide to use these jokes the most important thing is to have a fun no matter how groan worthy the Dad jokes may be.

HETA DAWSON   CORIN HEALY

# Classic Dad Jokes
## *Old, New and Totally Funny Dad Classics*

# TOTALLY AMAZING DAD JOKES

**Q. Have you tried this organic beer made of insects?**
A. I didn't like it, too hoppy

**Q. Wanna hear a plant joke?**
A. Oh sorry... I gotta leaf but I wood have liked to tell you.

**Q. Why did the invisible man turn down the job offer?**
A. Because he couldn't see himself doing it.

**Q. Why don't ants get ill?**
A. Because they have antibodies.

**Q. What is the difference between an alligator and a crocodile?**
A. One will see you later, and the other will see you in a while.

**Q. How did the farmer find his wife?**
A. He a-tractor.

**Q. What do you call a cow who is good at math?**
A Cow-culator.


**Q. Why was the coach yelling at a vending machine?**
A. He wanted his quarter back.


**Q. What do you call an elephant that no one wants?**
A. An irrelephant.


**Q. Did you hear about the power outlet who got into a fight with a power cord?**
A. He thought he could socket to him.


**Q. What do you call Santa's helpers?**
A. Subordinate clauses.

# TOTALLY AMAZING DAD JOKES

**Q. What do you call an elephant in a telephone booth?**
A. Stuck.

**Q. Why do Chickens not like the Internet?**
A. They prefer book, book, books.

**Q. Why did the Dad sell the vacuum cleaner?**
A. Because it was just gathering dust.

**Q. Why did the blind man fall into the well?**
A. Because he couldn't see that well.

**Q. Who do you call when you break your toe?**
A. A Toe Truck

**Q. What do you call a famous dad?**
A. POP star.


**Q. How many tickles does it take to make an octopus laugh?**
A. 10 tickles.


**Q. What did one Cowboy dad say to the other Cowboy dad?**
A. Live by the pun, die by the Pun.

**Q. Did you hear about the greedy clock?**
A. It went back four seconds.


**Q. What do you call an ant that has been shunned by his community?**
A. A socially dissed ant.


**Q. What do you call it when Batman skips Church?**
A. Christian Bale.

## TOTALLY AMAZING DAD JOKES

**Q. What did the buffalo say to his son when he dropped him off at school?**
A. "Bison."

**Q. Why do bees have sticky hair?**
A. Because they use Honeycombs.

**Q. Did you hear about the guy who invented Lifesavers?**
A. They say he made a mint!

**Q. What do you do if you kids want a space themed birthday party?**
A. You plan-et.

**Q. Why does a milking stool only have 4 legs?**
A. Because the cow has the utter one.

**Q. What do call a criminal landing an airplane?**
A. Condescending.

**Q. What's brown and sounds like a bell?**
A. Dung!

**Q. When does a joke become a dad joke?**
A. When it becomes apparent.

**Q. Why do trees seem suspicious on sunny days?**
A. They just seem a little shady!

## TOTALLY AMAZING DAD JOKES

**Q. What do you call a mac 'n' cheese that gets all up in your face?**
A. Too close for comfort food!

**Q. Why are aeroplanes so hard to see?**
A. Because they are in disguise.

**Q. How many storm troopers does it take to change a lightbulb?**
A. None. Because they are all on the dark side.

**Q. Why does Peter pan always fly?**
A. Because he neverlands!

**Q. Why do melons have weddings?**
A. Because they cantaloupe!

**Q. What do you get from a pampered cow?**
A. Spoiled milk.


**Q. How do make a music star out of a chicken?**
A. By making a chicken wrap.


**Q. What is so special about a shovel?**
A. It was a ground-breaking invention.


**Q. How much does it cost Santa to park his sleigh?**
A. Nothing, it's on the house.


**Q. Why can't bikes stand up on their own?**
A. Because they are two tyred.


**Q. What do seals do when they are feeling sick?**
A. They Sea Kelp.


**Q. Why can't dogs drive cars?**
A. Because they can't move it out of Bark.

## TOTALLY AMAZING DAD JOKES

**Q. Why did the wedding cake need a tissue?**
A. Because it was in tiers.

**Q. Why couldn't the toilet paper cross the road?**
A. Because it got stuck in the crack.

**Q. What was Beethoven's favourite fruit?**
A. The ba-na-na-na.

**Q. What did the mother broom say to the baby broom?**
A. It was time to go to sweep.

**Q. How does the moon cut its hair?**
A. Eclipse it.

**Q. What rock group has four men that don't sing?**
A. Mount Rushmore.

**Q. What time did the man go to the dentist?**
A. Tooth hurt-y.

**Q. Why did the coffee file a police report?**
A. It got mugged.


**Q. Why was the cookie very sad?**
A. It was feeling crumby.


**Q. What's the difference between a badly dressed man on a tricycle and a well-dressed man on a bicycle?**
A. Attire.


**Q. Dad, can you put the cat out?**
A. I didn't know it was on fire.


**Q. How much does a hipster weigh?**
A. An Instagram.


**Q. What kind of a car does an egg drive?**
A. A Yolkswagen.


**Q. Did you hear about the kidnapping at Pre-School?**
A. It's fine, he woke up.

# TOTALLY AMAZING DAD JOKES

**Q. Why did the green lettuce blush?**
A. It saw the salad dressing.


**Q. What day do you watch the Thor movies?**
A. Thors'day.


**Q. What is brown and sticky?**
A. A stick.


**Q. What time is it?**
A. I don't know. It keeps changing.


**Q. Don't you just hate it when people answer their own questions?**
A. I do.


**Q. What did the vegetarian priest say to the crowd?**
A. Lettuce pray!


**Q. What are you doing if you arrange squirrels by height?**
A. You are critter sizing.

**Q. What do you call someone who sees an Apple store get robbed?**
A. An iWitness.


**Q. Have you heard about the Italian chef who died?**
A. He pasta away.


**Q. What did the policeman say to his belly button?**
A. You're under a vest!


**Q. Want to hear a joke about newspaper?**
A. Never mind it's tearable.

# TOTALLY AMAZING DAD JOKES

**Q. What do you call a fly without wings?**
A. A walk.


**Q. Why are bananas considered sexy?**
A. Because there's sex-a-peel.


**Q. Why do you never hear a psychiatrist go to the toilet?**
A. Because the 'P' is silent.


**Q. What is so good about the earth rotating?**
A. It makes my day!


**Q. What did the fish say when he hit the wall?**
A. Dam.


**Q. Why is it so hard to work out what species birds are?**
A. Because they are always in da-skies.


**Q. My daughter screeched, "Daaaaaad, you haven't listened to one word I've said, have you!?**
A. What a strange way to start a conversation with me!

**Q. How many apples grow on a tree?**
A. All of them of course!


**Q. How many contractors does it take to change a lightbulb?**
A. Ohhhhhhh, hard to say, looks like a big job, when we get the light bulb out, could be all sorts of problems.


**Q. Do you know the story about the chicken that crossed the Mexican border?**
A. Me neither, I couldn't follow it.


**Q. What do you call a reindeer with no eyes and no legs?**
A. Still no idea.

## TOTALLY AMAZING DAD JOKES

**Q. What does a house wear?**
A. A dress.

**Q. As a lumberjack I know I have chopped down 3,123 trees. How you ask?**
A. Every time I chop one down, I keep a log.

**Q. What do you call someone who steps on a cornflake?**
A. Cereal killer.

**Q. What do you call a Mexican whose vehicle has been stolen?**
A. Carlos.

**Q. How do you make a handkerchief dance?**
A. You put a little boogie in it.

**Q. What do you call a man with a spade on his head?**
A. Dug.

**Q. Why do bees hum?**
A. Because they don't know the words.

**Q. What's the best smelling insect?**
A. A deodar-ant.

**Q. How do you help a crocodile if it gets injured?**
A. Give it Gatorade.

**Q. What's a ninja's favorite type of shoes?**
A. Sneakers!

## TOTALLY AMAZING DAD JOKES

**Q. Did you hear about the guy who stole calendars?**
A. He got 12 months.


**Q. I was wondering "Why does a frisbee appear larger the closer it gets?"**
A. And then it hit me!


**Q. What do you call the graveyard in town?**
A. The dead centre of town.


**Q. Is this pool safe for diving?**
A. It deep ends.


**Q. What is the cutest creature in the sea?**
A. A cuddlefish.


**Q. What birds do you find in Portugal?**
A. Portugeese.


**Q. Why didn't the two roosters cross the road?**
A. They were too chicken.

**Q. What did the Dad name his son who was born in the car on the way to the hospital?**
A. Carson


**Q. What does a vegetarian zombie eat?**
A. GRA-A-A-A-A-I-I-I-I-N-N-N-S-S


**Q. How can you spot a Dogwood tree?**
A. By its Bark!


**Q. What did the mathematician say to the person who created the zero?**
A. Thanks for nothing.


**Q. What did the picture say to the wall?**
A. First they frame me than they hang me.


**Q. What happens when you make too many right hand turns in life?**
A. You'll get dizzy.


**Q. What type of bagel can fly?**
A. A plane bagel.

# TOTALLY AMAZING DAD JOKES

**Q. Why do some couples go to the gym?**
A. Because some relationships don't work out.

**Q. Why is it terrible to work in a shoe recycling shop?**
A. Because it is sole destroying.

**Q. Why did the angler dress up in a suit to go fishing?**
A. He was fishing for a compliment.

**Q. Dad, did you get a haircut?**
A. No, I got them all cut!

**Q. Why do scuba divers fall backwards out of the boat?**
A. Because if they fall frontwards...they'd still be in the boat.

**Q. Why don't roofs sing?**
A. They're too pitchy.

**Q. What language do dandruff speak?**
A. Hairbrew!


**Q. Which Spice Girl can carry the most petrol?**
A. Geri can.


**Q. Why did the math book look so sad?**
A. Because of all of its problems!


**Q. What did the computer go to the doctor?**
A. Because he had a virus!


**Q. You are on a horse riding full gallop. Next to you is a giraffe at full gallop. behind you is a lion on your tail. What do you do?**
A. Get off the carousel.


**Q. How does a computer learn something?**
A. Bit, by bit, by bit.


**Q. Why do doctors hit people knees with their little hammer?**
A. Because they get a kick out of it.

## TOTALLY AMAZING DAD JOKES

**Q. How does a Penguin make a house for itself?**
A. Igloos it together.

**Q. What did the ocean say to the seashore?**
A. Nothing, it gave a big wave!

**Q. Why don't dinosaurs talk?**
A. Because they're dead.

**Q. What do you get when you cross an elephant and a rhino?**
A. El-eph-ino!

**Q. What do you call it when you cannot go pee?**
A. Urine trouble.

**Q. When does an arborist finish work?**
A. At tree o'clock.

**Q. Did you hear about the cannibal who threw a pile of funny bones into a boiling pot?**
A. He made himself a laughingstock.

**Q. Which country's capital city has the fastest-growing population?**
A. Ireland. Every day it's Dublin.

**Q. Why do people pick their nose?**
A. Because they don't like the one they were born with.

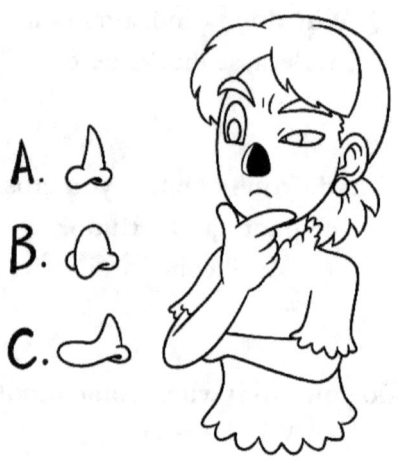

**Q. Why did the can crusher quit his job?**
A. Because it was soda pressing!

**Q. Which state has the most streets?**
A. Rhode Island.

# TOTALLY AMAZING DAD JOKES

**Q. What do you call cheese that isn't yours?**
A. Nacho cheese.


**Q. How do you get a squirrel to like you?**
A. Act like a nut.


**Q. Did you hear that McDonalds now have burgers patties made from insects?**

A. They call it a Hoppy Meal.


**Q. What do you call an airplane with no wings?**
A. Air Plain.


**Q. Why did the coffee taste like dirt?**
A. because it was GROUND just a couple minutes ago.


**Q. Did you know diarrhea is hereditary?**
A. It runs in your genes.

**Q. Are you ready for the zoom meeting?**
A. Not even remotely.

**Q. How do you light up a football stadium?**
A. With a football match.


**Q. Why are spiders so smart?**
A. They can find everything on the web.


**Q. How does Moses make his coffee?**
A. Hebrews it.


**Q. What did the left eye say to the right eye?**
A. Between us, something smells.

# TOTALLY AMAZING DAD JOKES

**Q. Did you hear about the explosion at the cheese factory?**
A. There was de brie everywhere!


**Q. What do you call a man who can't stand up?**
A. Neil.


**Q. How do moths swim?**
A. Using the butterfly stroke.


**Q. What do you call a sink with a shoe in it?**
A. A clogged sink.


**Q. What did the fisherman say to the magician?**
A. Pick a cod, any cod.


**Q. Why is having a cross eyed teacher an issue?**
A. Because she can't control her pupils.


**Q. Which is faster, hot or cold?**
A. Hot, because you can catch a cold.

**Q. Why did the Mexican man push his wife off a cliff?**
A. Tequila


**Q. Why did the baker steal a mixer from work?**
A. It was a whisk he was willing to take.


**Q. How do you stop a baby lettuce from crying?**
A. Rock it.


**Q. What do you call it when a hen looks at a lettuce?**
A. A chicken ceasar salad.


**Q. What do you call a Dad joke that no one laughs at?**
A. A Dead joke.

# TOTALLY AMAZING DAD JOKES

**Q. What do you call an illegally parked frog?**
A. Toad.

**Q. What's a Dads favourite chair?**
A. A recliner, it's because they go way back.

**Q. Why did the egg have a day off?**
A. because it was Fryday.

**Q. Why is Saturday stronger than Wednesday?**
A. Wednesday is a week day.

**Q. How do Lawyers say goodbye?**
A. We'll be suing ya!

**Q. What do scholars eat when they're hungry?**
A. Academia nuts.

**Q. Why did the boy eat his homework?**
A. Because his teacher said it was a piece of cake.

**Q. What is a cannibals favourite food?**
A. Raw-men.

**Q. What do you call a really fat psychic?**
A. A four chin teller.

## TOTALLY AMAZING DAD JOKES

**Q. Why is making a diamond shaped like a duck a bad idea?**
A. It quacks under pressure.

**Q. Why was the cheese sad?**
A. Because it was Blue!

**Q. Why did the pony ask for a glass of water?**
A. Because he was a little horse.

**Q. What is a cats favourite pizza?**
A. Purrrrperoni.

**Q. Why was the graveyard overcrowded?**
A. Because people are dying to get there.

**Q. Can February March?**
A. No, but April May.

**Q. Did you hear about the cafe on the moon?**
A. Great food, no atmosphere.

**Q. What do you call a woman who sounds like an ambulance?**
A. Nina.


**Q. Want to hear my pizza joke?**
A. Never mind, it's too cheesy.


**Q. What do you call an alligator wearing a vest?**
A. An investi-gator.


**Q. What do you call someone with no body and no nose?**
A. Nobody knows.


**Q. What word can you make shorter by adding two letters?**
A. Short!


**Q. What did the scarf say to the hat?**
A. "You hang around here, I'll go on ahead".

## TOTALLY AMAZING DAD JOKES

**Q. Why are skeletons so calm?**
A. Because nothing gets under their skin!

**Q. What do they call Miley Cyrus in Europe?**
A. Kilometry Cyprus.

**Q. What do enemies and enemas have in common?**
A. They are both a pain in the butt.

**Q. What do you call pie?**
A. Yummy.

**Q. What are a bee's favourite neckless made from?**
A. Bee-ds.

**Q. Hey is your refrigerator running?**
A. You better go catch it.

**Q. What do you call a fake noodle?**
A. An Impasta.

**Q. What do you call a cow that just had a baby calf?**
A. A New Moother

**Q. What do you call a can of soup that eats other cans of soup?**
A. A CANnibal.

**Q. What fish can you use to make your car go faster?**
A. A tuna.

# TOTALLY AMAZING DAD JOKES

**Q. What is it, when you have a bear with no teeth?**
A. A Gummy Bear!

**Q. What did one light bulb say to the other at a party?**
A. "This party's lit".

**Q. Why don't eggs tell jokes?**
A. They'd crack each other up.

**Q. Why did the turkey cross the road TWICE?**
A. To prove he wasn't a chicken.

**Q: What has four wheels and flies?**
A: A garbage truck!

**Q. Why did the scarecrow win an award?**
A. Because he was outstanding in his field.

**Q. What's the skeletons favorite road?**
A. Dead end!

**Q. What letter in the alphabet has the most water?**
A. C.

**Q. What did the janitor say when he jumped out of the broom closet?**
A. Supplies!!!!

**Q. What do you call a rabbit with fleas?**
A. "bugs" bunny.

**Q. Why did the chicken cross the road?**
A. It was bored of just standing there.

## TOTALLY AMAZING DAD JOKES

**Q. What do Santa's elves listen to ask they work?**
A. Wrap music!

**Q. How many South Americans does it take to change a lightbulb?**
A. A Brazilian.

**Q. Did you hear about the truck carrying sheep carcasses that crashed?**
A. Locals said it was offal.

**Q. What do the secret service yell when protecting the President?**
A. Donald, duck!

**Q. Did you hear about the man who was sacked from the calendar factory?**
A. He took a couple of days off.

**Q. Why do seagulls fly over the ocean?**
A. Because if they flew over the bay we'd call them bagels.

**Q. What happened when you go on a tropical food diet?**
A. It makes a mango crazy.


**Q. What Happened to the boiling water?**
A. It will be mist.


**Q. Why are bananas good at drag racing?**
A. Because they like to peel out of places.


**Q. What do you call the boss at Old MacDonald's Farm?**
A. The CIEIO


**Q. What would you call Thor if he wrote a novel?**
A. and Au-Thor


**Q. Why don't skeletons ever go trick or treating?**
A. Because they have no body to go with.

## TOTALLY AMAZING DAD JOKES

**Q. What do you call a factory that sells passable products?**
A. A satisfactory!

**Q. What is a cow that just had a baby?**
A. De-CALF-einated

**Q. Did you hear about the circus fire?**
A. It was in tents.

**Q. What do you call a man with a seagull on his head?**
A. You call him 'Cliff.'

**Q. Why do crabs never give to charity?**
A. Because they're shellfish.

**Q. Why didn't the skeleton climb the mountain?**
A. It didn't have the guts!

**Q. Why did the whale cross the harbour?**
A. To get to the other tide.

**Q. What happens when a drummer comes out of retirement?**
A. There are repercussions.

**Q. Have you ever seen me tie my shoelaces with my mind?**
A. I thought knot

**Q. What's a foot long and slippery?**
A. A slipper.

# TOTALLY AMAZING DAD JOKES

**Q. Guess what I saw?**
A. Wood


**Q. What do sprinters eat before a race?**
A. Nothing, they fast!


**Q. Why was the cook arrested?**
A. He was caught beating an egg.


**Q. What do you call an intelligent Genie?**
A. A Genius

**Q. Where do baby cats learn to swim?**
A. The kitty pool.


**Q. What did one wall say to the other?**
A. I'll meet you at the corner.


**Q. Why did the lollipop store close down?**
A. They lost their licker license.


**Q. Why did the elephant stand on the marshmallow?**
A. So he wouldn't fall into the hot chocolate.


**Q. How can a leopard change his spots?**
A. By moving.


**Q. What do you call a deer with no eyes?**
A. No idea.


**Q. Did you hear the rumor about butter?**
A. Well, I'm not going to spread it!

## TOTALLY AMAZING DAD JOKES

**Q. Where do you see yourself in 5 years?**
A. In a mirror.

**Q. What did the tomato say to the other tomato during a race?**
A. You had better Ketch up.

**Q. What did the guy say when he got caught downloading the entire Wikipedia?**
A. I can explain everything.

**Q. What is a witches favorite topic?**
A. Spelling!

**Q. Why shouldn't you eat Sushi?**
A. It's a little bit fishy

**Q. What's an astronaut's favorite part of a computer?**
A. The SPACE bar.

**Q.** Why are snakes measured in inches?
A. Because they don't have any feet.


**Q.** What did Hannibal Lecter call his imaginary friend?
A. Stu.


**Q.** Where did the general keep his armies?
A. In his Sleevies!


**Q.** Want to hear a joke about construction?
A. Nah, I'm still working on it.


**Q.** What do you call it when you go drifting in a Tesla?
A. Electric slide.


**Q.** What did the baby corn say to the mama corn?
A. Where's POP corn?

## TOTALLY AMAZING DAD JOKES

**Q. Why can't a nose be 12 inches long?**
A. Because then it would be a foot.


**Q. Why do chicken coops have two doors?**
A. Because if they had four doors, they'd be chicken sedans.


**Q. What did the sushi say to the bee?**
A. Wasabi.


**Q. What's the best way to watch a fly-fishing tournament?**
A. Live stream.


**Q. Dad "What's the difference between a piano, a tuna, and a pot of glue? Kid "I don't know"?**
A. You can tuna piano, but you can't piano a tuna.
Kid "What about the glue?
Dad "I knew you would get stuck there"


**Q. Why can't you hear a pterodactyl using the bathroom?**
A. Because the P is silent.

**Q. What's the quickest way to double your money?**
A. Fold it in half.


**Q. What's the heaviest soup in Asia?**
A. One ton.


**Q. Why do you never see elephants hiding in trees?**
A. Because they're so good at it.


**Q. What does the cell say to his sister when she steps on his toe?**
A. "Oh my toe sis!"


**Q. Who can drink 5 litres of gasoline?**
A. Jerry can!


**Q. What's Forrest Gump's Facebook password?**
A. 1forest1


**Q. How do you tell the difference between a bull and a milk cow?**
A. It is either one or the utter.

## TOTALLY AMAZING DAD JOKES

**Q. How do celebrities stay cool?**
A. They have many fans.

**Q. What do you call someone who moves beehives in America?**
A. A US Bee driver.

**Q. Son: Dad, how does it feel to have an amazing son?**
A. Dad: I don't know, ask your grandfather!

**Q. Why was the broom late for work?**
A. It overswept!

**Q. Did you hear about the electric eel who went to the hospital?**
A. She was discharged.

**Q. Why would you hire a Duck detective?**
A. Because you know that he will Quack the case.

**Q. What do you call a pile of cats?**
A. A meowtain.

**Q. Why can't a leopard hide?**
A. Because he's always spotted.

**Q. Why can you trust a walrus to keep a secret?**
A. Because his lips are sealed.

**Q. Have you heard about the new movie called constipated?**
A. Oh wait...it hasn't come out yet.

## TOTALLY AMAZING DAD JOKES

**Q. Why should you not do dad jokes about retired people?**
A. None of them work.


**Q. Why are elevator jokes so good?**
A. They work on so many levels.


**Q. Did you know that Davy Crockett had three ears?**
A. His left ear, his right ear and his wild frontier.


**Q. What kind of fish is made of only 2 sodium atoms?**
A. 2 Na


**Q. What do you call a man who won't fart in public?**
A. A private tutor!


**Q. What do you call a cow with a twitch?**
A. Beef jerky.

**Q. What is a hairdresser's favourite food?**
A. Barber-que of course.


**Q. What did the pirate say on his 80th birthday?**
A. Aye matey!


**Q. Did I tell you the time I fell in love during a backflip?**
A. I was heels overhead.


**Q. We're do boats go when there sick?**
A. The boat doc.


**Q. Have you heard about these amazing new property investment opportunities in Egypt?**
A. Don't do it, it's a pyramid scheme.


**Q. What do you call a Cowboy Dad?**
A. A Punslinger!


**Q. What do you call an eyeless fish?**
A. Fsh.

## TOTALLY AMAZING DAD JOKES

**Q. Have you heard about the chocolate record player?**
A. It sounds pretty sweet.

**Q. What do you call a man with no arms and no legs stuffed in your mailbox?**
A. Bill!

**Q. What do you call a super articulate dinosaur?**
A Thesaurus.

**Q. Why are dogs horrible dancers?**
A. Because they have two left feet!

**Q. How was Rome split in two?**
A. With a pair of Caesar's.

**Q. What does a baby computer call its father?**
A. Data.

**Q. Why are colds bad criminals?**
A. Because they're easy to catch.

**Q. What grades did the pirate get on his report card?**
A. Seven Cs

**Q. When is a door not really a door?**
A. When it's really ajar.

**Q. Why do vampires seem sick?**
A. They're always coffin.

**Q. What do you call a person missing 75% of their spine?**
A. A quarter back.

**Q. What does a storm cloud wear under his raincoat?**
A. Thunderwear.

**Q. What would you get if you'd put a lawyer in a suit?**
A. A lawsuit.

## TOTALLY AMAZING DAD JOKES

**Q. How does a cucumber become a pickle?**
A. It goes through a jarring experience.

**Q. What are two structures that hold water?**
A. Well, Damn...I just can't think of any.

**Q. Why is it a hard decision to be an organ donor?**
A. Because it takes guts.

**Q. What happens when you go to the bathroom in France?**
A. European.

**Q. Did you hear about the bacon cheeseburger who couldn't stop telling jokes?**
A. It was on a roll.

**Q. Why is it hard to see a camel in the dessert?**
A. Because they are camelflaged.

**Q. How did the cows change paddocks?**
A. They were moooved.


**Q. Why did the coroner go to the hairdresser?**
A. He heard someone dyed there


**Q. What did the Prison Libarian think of his job?**
A. It had its prose and cons.

TOTALLY AMAZING DAD JOKES

## Knock, Knock Jokes

Knock, knock.
Who's there?
Keanu.
Keanu who?
Keanu let me in, it's cold out here!

Knock, knock.
Who's there?
Sherwood.
Sherwood who?
Sherwood like you to open the door!

Knock, knock.
Who's there?
Voodoo.
Voodoo who?
Voodoo you think you are, asking me so many questions?

Knock, knock.
Who's there?
Billy Bob Joe Penny.
Billy Bob Joe Penny who?
Really? How many Billy Bob Joe Pennies do you know?

Knock, knock.
Who's there?
Spell.
Spell who?
Okay, fine. W-H-O.

## TOTALLY AMAZING DAD JOKES

Knock, knock.
Who's there?
Ivor.
Ivor who?
Ivor you let me in or I'll climb through the window.

Knock, knock.
Who's there?
Déjà.
Déjà who?
Knock, knock.

Knock, knock.
Who's there?
Lettuce.
Lettuce who?
Lettuce in it's cold out here.

Knock, knock
Who's There?
Ash
Ash who?
Bless you!

Knock, knock
Who's there?
Nobel
Nobel who?
No bell, that's why I knocked!

## HETA DAWSON   CORIN HEALY

Knock, knock
Who's there?
Leaf
Leaf who?
Leaf me alone!

Knock, knock
Who's there?
Tank
Tank Who?
You're welcome!

Knock, knock
Who's There?
Who
Who Who?
Is there an owl in there?

Knock, knock
Who's There?
Theodore
Theodore who?
Theodore is stuck and it won't open!

Knock, knock
Who's There?
Amos
Amos who?
A mosquito bit me!

## TOTALLY AMAZING DAD JOKES

Knock, knock.
Who's there?
Interrupting Cow.
Interrupting c— Moooo!

Knock, knock.
Who's there?
Dwayne.
Dwayne who?
Dwayne the bathtub already. I'm drowning!

Knock, knock.
Who's there?
Candice.
Candice who?
Candice joke get any worse?!

Knock, knock.
Who's there?
Hatch.
Hatch who?
God bless you.

Knock, knock.
Who's there?
Kenya.
Kenya who?
Kenya feel the love tonight?

## HETA DAWSON   CORIN HEALY

Knock, knock
Who's there?
Beef
Beef who?
Before I get cold, you'd better let me in!

Knock, knock.
Who's there?
Smellmop.
Smellmop who?
Ew, no thanks!

Knock, knock.
Who's there?
Justin
Justin who?
Justin the neighborhood, thought I'd drop by.

Knock, knock.
Who's there?
A leaf.
A leaf who?
A leaf you alone if you leaf me alone.

Knock, knock.
Who's there?
Dishes!
Dishes who?
Dishes the Police come out with your hands up.

## TOTALLY AMAZING DAD JOKES

Knock, knock.
Who's there?
Kanga.
Kanga who?
Actually, it's kangaroo!

Knock, knock.
Who's there?
Robin.
Robin who?
Robin you, now hand over the cash!

Knock, knock.
Who's there?
Cargo.
Cargo who?
No, car go "beep beep"!

Knock, knock.
Who's there?
Luke.
Luke who?
Luke through the the peep hole and find out.

Knock, knock.
Who's there?
Theodore.
Theodore who?
Theodore wasn't opened so I knocked.

## HETA DAWSON   CORIN HEALY

Knock, knock.
Who's there?
Wooden shoe.
Wooden shoe who?
Wooden shoe like to know!

Knock, knock.
Who's there?
Turnip.
Turnip who?
Turnip the volume, I love this song!

Knock, knock.
Who's there?
Closure.
Closure who?
Closure mouth while you're chewing!

Knock, knock.
Who's there?
Andrew!
Andrew who?
Andrew a picture!

Knock, knock.
Who's there?
Nun.
Nun who?
Nunya business!

## TOTALLY AMAZING DAD JOKES

Knock, knock.
Who's there?
Alex.
Alex who?
Alex-plain when you open the door!

Knock, knock.
Who's there?
Figs.
Figs who?
Figs the doorbell, it's broken!

Knock, knock.
Who's there?
Noise.
Noise who?
Noise to see you!

Knock, knock.
Who's there?
Oswald.
Oswald who?
Oswald my bubble gum!

Knock, knock.
Who's there?
Ida.
Ida who?
Surely, it's pronounced Idaho.

Knock, knock.
Who's there?
Candice.
Candice who?
Candice door open or what?

Knock, knock.
Who's there?
Cereal.
Cereal who?
Cereal pleasure to meet you!

Knock, knock.
Who's there?
Cantaloupe!
Cantaloupe who?
Cantaloupe to Vegas, our parents would get mad.

Knock, knock.
Who's there?
Annie.
Annie who?
Annie way you can let me in now?

Knock, knock.
Who's there?
A little old lady.
A little old lady who?
Dang! All this time, I had no idea you could yodel.

## TOTALLY AMAZING DAD JOKES

Knock, knock.
Who's there?
Tyrone.
Tyrone who?
Tyrone shoelaces!

Knock, knock.
Who's there?
Keith!
Keith who?
Keith me, my thweet preenth!

Knock, knock.
Who's there?
Mustache.
Mustache who?
Mustache you a question, but I'll shave it for later

Knock, knock.
Who's there?
Art.
Art who?
Art 2-D2!

Knock, knock.
Who's there?
Snow.
Snow who?
Snow use. I forgot my name again!

Knock, knock.
Who's there?
Cook.
Cook who?
Yeah, you do sound crazy!

Knock, knock.
Who's there?
Lion.
Lion who?
Lion on your doorstep, open up!

Knock, knock.
Who's there?
Butter.
Butter who?
Butter be quick. I have to go to the bathroom!

Knock, knock.
Who's there?
Police.
Police who?
Police stop telling these awful knock knock jokes!

Knock, knock.
Who's there?
Donut.
Donut who?
Donut ask, it's a secret!

## TOTALLY AMAZING DAD JOKES

Knock, knock.
Who's there?
Says.
Says who?
Says me, that's who!

Knock, knock.
Who's there?
Bruce.
Bruce who?
I Bruce easily, don't hit me!

Knock, knock.
Who's there?
Ice cream.
Ice cream who?
Ice cream if you don't let me inside!

Knock, knock.
Who's there?
Canoe.
Canoe who?
Canoe come and play?
I'm bored!

Knock, knock.
Who's there?
Nana.
Nana who?
Nana your business.

Knock, knock.
Who's there?
Ice cream soda.
Ice cream soda who?
Ice scream soda people can hear me!

Knock, knock.
Who's there?
Amish.
Amish who?
Really, you're a shoe? Uh, okay.

Knock, knock.
Who's there?
I am.
I am who?
Don't you even know who you are?!

Knock, knock.
Who's there?
Iran.
Iran who?
Iran all the way here!

Knock, knock.
Who's there?
Boo.
Boo who?
Hey, don't cry!

## TOTALLY AMAZING DAD JOKES

Knock, knock.
Who's there?
Pecan!
Pecan who?
Pecan somebody your own size!

Knock, knock.
Who's there?
Cash.
Cash who?
No thanks, but I'd love some peanuts!

Knock, knock.
Who's there?
Yah.
Yah who?
No thanks, I use Bing or Google.

Knock, knock.
Who's there?
An extra-terrestrial.
An extra-terrestrial who?
Wait, how many extra-terrestrials do you know?

Knock, knock.
Who's there?
Gorilla.
Gorilla who?
Gorilla me a hamburger.

Knock, knock.
Who's there?
Adore.
Adore who?
Adore is between you and me so please open up!

Knock, knock.
Who's there?
Icing.
Icing who?
Icing so loud, the neighbors can hear.

Knock, knock.
Who's there?
Hike.
Hike who?
I didn't know you liked Japanese poetry!

Knock, knock.
Who's there?
FBI.
FBI w- We're asking the questions here.

Knock, knock.
Who's there?
Sarah.
Sarah who?
Sa-rah phone I could use?

## TOTALLY AMAZING DAD JOKES

Knock, knock.
Who's there?
Daisy.
Daisy who?
Daisy me rollin, they hatin'.

Knock, knock.
Who's there?
Control Freak.
Okay, now you say, "Control Freak who?!"

Knock, knock.
Who's there?
Les.
Les who?
Les go out!

Knock, knock.
Who's there?
Anita.
Anita who?
Anita go to the bathroom!

Knock, knock.
Who's there?
Water.
Water who?
Water you waiting for, open the door!

Knock, knock.
Who's there?
Anita.
Anita who?
Anita drink of water so please let me in!

Knock, knock.
Who's there?
Ho-ho..
Ho-ho who?
Your Santa impression needs work.

Knock, knock.
Who's there?
A Mayan.
A Mayan who?
A Mayan in the way?

Knock, knock.
Who's there?
Opportunity.
Opportunity doesn't knock twice!

Knock, knock.
Who's there?
Mikey.
Mikey who?
Mikey is missing, can you please open up!

## TOTALLY AMAZING DAD JOKES

Knock, knock.
Who's there?
Doctor.
Doctor who?
No, no, just the doctor.

Knock, knock.
Who's there?
A broken pencil.
A broken pencil who?
Never mind it's pointless

Knock, knock.
Who's there?
Hawaii.
Hawaii who?
I'm fine, Hawaii you?

Knock, knock.
Who's there?
Max.
Max who?
Max no difference, open the door!

Knock, knock.
Who's there?
Alpaca.
Alpaca who?
Alpaca the trunk, you pack the suitcase.

## HETA DAWSON   CORIN HEALY

Knock, knock.
Who's there?
Ben.
Ben who?
Ben hoping I can come in!

Knock, knock.
Who's there?
Olive.
Olive who?
Olive you and I don't care who knows it!

Knock, knock.
Who's there?
Amos.
Amos who?
A mosquito!

Knock, knock.
Who's there?
Major.
Major who?
Major day with this joke haven't I?

Knock, knock.
Who's there?
Aida.
Aida who?
Aida sandwich for lunch today.

## TOTALLY AMAZING DAD JOKES

Knock, knock.
Who's there? Razor.
Razor who?
Razor hand and dance the boogie!

Knock, knock.
Who's there?
Leon.
Leon who?
🎵Leon me, when you're not strong. 🎵

Knock, knock.
Who's there?
Euripides.
Euripides who?
Euripides jeans, you pay for 'em.

Knock, knock.
Who's there?
The Chicken
The Chicken who?
The Chicken who crossed the road to get here

Knock knock
Who's there?
Cows
Cows who?
No, cows go moo

HETA DAWSON   CORIN HEALY

# Dad one-liners
*So Bad you will want Dad to stop*

## TOTALLY AMAZING DAD JOKES

**I am terrified of elevators...**
I am going to be taking steps to avoid them!


**I quit my job as a hairdresser...**
It was too cut and dry!


**I had a job predicting lightning storms...**
I went on strike!


**Kid: "I'm hungry."**
Dad: " Hi, Hungry, I'm Dad"


**I refused to believe that my dad was stealing from his job as a road worker.**
But when I went round to his house,
all the signs were there!


**Whoever invented "Knock-knock" jokes...**
should get a no-bell prize!


**I ain't going vegan...**
It'd be a missed steak!

## HETA DAWSON   CORIN HEALY

**Two cannibals are eating a clown,**
**One says to the other...**
"Does this taste funny to you?"


**So a vowel saves another vowel's life...**
The other vowel says, "Aye E! I owe you!"


**I tried to be a swimsuit model...**
too much exposure!


**Whenever the cashier at the grocery store asks my dad if he would like the milk in a bag he replies,**
"No, just leave it in the carton!"


**I accidentally dropped my pillow on the floor...**
I think it has a con-cushion!


**I fired my electrician...**
His work shocked me!

**I was sitting in traffic the other day...**
Probably why I got run over!

## TOTALLY AMAZING DAD JOKES

**I'm reading a book about anti-gravity...**
It's impossible to put down!

**Two wind turbines stand in a field. One says to the other, "So, what kind of music are you into?"**
The other replies, "I'm a huge metal fan."

**A pair of jump leads walk into a pub. The barman tells them…**
"I'll serve you, but don't go starting anything."

**I told my kids not to bite the hand
that feeds them…**
They said that they would never bite their mother!


**I had a neck brace fitted years ago…**
And I've never looked back since!


**I quit my job as a dog walker…**
The feedback I got was rough!


**I wouldn't buy anything with Velcro…**
It's a total rip-off!


**I had to sell my haemophiliac dog…**
He wouldn't heal!


**I used to get electric shocks from touching
a door handle but it hasn't happened for a while…**
I am ex-static!


**I'm on a special diet. It's a sea food diet…**
I see food and I eat it!

## TOTALLY AMAZING DAD JOKES

**A man walked into a bar...**
Ouch!

**Thanks for explaining the word "many" to me...**
It means a lot!

**Do you know scientists freshen their breath?**
With experi-mints!

**Dad: It said on the news that an actress has stabbed someone. Think her name was Reese.**
Mum: Witherspoon? Dad: No, with a knife!

## HETA DAWSON   CORIN HEALY

**I don't play soccer because I enjoy the sport.**
I'm just doing it for kicks!


**My arborist did a terrible job and I wanted my money back...**
He said I should speak to the branch manager!


**My friend is a terrible stand-up comedian...**
He tells jokes about the meat works... they are just offal


**I quit my job as an electrician...**
I just lost the spark!


**My best friend slept through a burglary...**
He was a terrible getaway driver!


**So, I came home from work yesterday to find that someone broke into my apartment. Looking around, it seemed like they didn't really take a whole lot. My TV was still there, my PS4, and my Legos were fine. But the apartment was dark, even when I tried to turn on the lights. Seems the only thing that was taken were my lightbulbs and a couple lamps...**
I was delighted!

# TOTALLY AMAZING DAD JOKES

**"Doctor, I keep seeing an insect buzzing around me."**
"Don't worry; that's just a bug that's going around."


**It's a 5-minute walk from my house to the pub,
It's a 35-minute walk from the pub to my house**...
The difference is staggering!


**Conjunctivitis.com...**
now that's a site for sore eyes!


**You can't run through a camp site...**
You can only ran, because it's past tents!


**I saw a guy in the supermarket wearing a robe...**
he comes up to me and says,
"hey, why are you wearing a robe"


**People say I am stubborn...**
But I never believe them!


**My new thesaurus is terrible...**
Not only that, but it's also terrible!

## HETA DAWSON   CORIN HEALY

**I met some obsessive chess players in a hotel reception going on about how good they are…**
They were chess-nuts boasting in an open foyer!


**If at first you don't succeed…**
Skydiving is not for you!


**"What did Mississippi let Delaware?"**
"I don't know, but Alaska!


**Within minutes, the detectives knew what the murder weapon was…**
It was a briefcase!

**I hate perforated lines,**
They are tearable!

## TOTALLY AMAZING DAD JOKES

**I can't stop stealing.
Sometimes when it gets really bad...**
I take something for it!


**When it comes to buying property,
they say it's too expensive in New York.**
Not if it's your burial plot!


**A cartoonist has been found dead...**
Details are sketchy!


**Dad, are we pyromaniacs**
Yes, we arson!


**As a fugitive I did a lot of jogging...**
I was tired of running!


**My wife doesn't appreciate my dad jokes...**
She said they are punishing!


**Lots of cars in a multi- storey car park
have been broken into...**
That's wrong on so many levels!

### HETA DAWSON  CORIN HEALY

**Which U.S. state is famous for it's extra-small soft drinks?**
Minnesota!


**What happens if you punch a frequency?**
It Hertz!


**I'd like to give a big shout out to all the sidewalks...**
For keeping me off the streets!


**I named my horse Mayo...**
Mayo neighs!


**I recently crashed a yacht...**
It keeled over!


**What's orange and sounds like a Parrot?**
A Carrot!


**A Dad is washing his car with his son.**
The son says: "Dad, can't you use a sponge?"

# TOTALLY AMAZING DAD JOKES

**I had seafood last night...**
Now I'm eel!

**I was going to tell a time-traveling joke...**
But you guys didn't like it!

**I told my wife she was drawing her eyebrows too high...**
She looked surprised!

**Son: "Where are my sunglasses?"**
Dad: I don't know...where are my dad glasses?

## HETA DAWSON    CORIN HEALY

**My wife is really mad at the fact that I have no sense of direction…**
So, I packed up my stuff and right!


**I had to take my cat to the vet as this new iron rich food was making him sick…**
Turns out he was faking, he was feline!


**Dad: Can I administer my own anaesthetic?**
Surgeon: Go ahead - knock yourself out.!


**I've never gone to a gun range before…**
So, I decided to give it a shot!


**I tried a new sport, axe throwing…**
I quit, they said I was too wooden!


**I am making a list of reasons to move to Switzerland…**
The Flag is a big plus!


**An actress got a part playing a very small mother….**
She was paid the minimum wage!

# TOTALLY AMAZING DAD JOKES

**A restaurant tried serving me a custard that had gone off...**
I complained and said I was dis-custard!

**When I was a kid, my Dad told me I could be anyone I wanted to be...**
Turns out, identity theft is a crime!

**"Hey Dad, I was thinking..."**
"I thought I smelled something burning."

**We have enough youth…**
How about a Fountain of Smart?

**I left my job as a smartphone reviewer…**
I wasn't comparing apples with apples!

**I tripped over my wife's bra…**
It appeared to be a booby trap!

**They say that 'Money talks'…**
But all mine ever says is 'goodbye!'.

## TOTALLY AMAZING DAD JOKES

**Yesterday I saw a dwarf prisoner climbing down a wall…**
I thought to myself, "now that's a little condescending"

**I went on a once-in-a-lifetime vacation...**
Never again!

**I saw an ad that said "radio for sale $2, volume stuck on full"**
I thought to myself "I can't turn that down".

**Two TV aerials got married...**
The ceremony was boring, but the reception was amazing!

**A Dutchman has invented shoes that record how many miles you've walked…**
Clever clogs!.

**I tell my kids to follow their dreams…**
Now it's just an excuse for them to sleep all day!

**After dinner, I was asked if I could clear the table…**
I needed a run up, but I made it!


**Two guys walk into a bar…**
The third guy ducks!

**I was just reminiscing about the beautiful herb garden I had when I was growing up…**
Good thymes!


**David left his ID on the train….**
We now call him Dav!


**Someone's broke into the boot of my wife's car…**
but don't worry, it was an open and shut case!


**I gave my dad his 50th birthday card…**
He said: "One would have been enough."


**I just finished making my first bookcase…**
I'm very proud of my shelf!

# TOTALLY AMAZING DAD JOKES

**I quit my job as an upholsterer...**
It wouldn't cover the bills...

**"How far away is dinner?"**
"About two metres."

**I made a pencil with two erasers...**
It was pointless!

**Elvis Presley couldn't write a song after experiencing an earthquake...**
He was all shook up!

**I got a hen to regularly count her own eggs...**
She's a real mathamachicken!

**I ate a clock today...**
It was very time-consuming!

**I'm starting a new dating service in Prague...**
It's called Czech-Mate!

**I used to buy and sell used prosthetics...**
I was an arms dealer!

**My friend met his wife with a dating app...**
You could say it was love at first swipe!

**I had a falling out with our neighbours recently, someone put a hole in the fence...**
they got sick of me looking into it!

**I'm addicted to collecting vintage Beatles albums...**
I need Help!

**To whoever stole my copy of Microsoft Office,**
I will find you. You have my Word!

**I lost my job as a philosopher...**
I try not to think about it!

# TOTALLY AMAZING DAD JOKES

**I bought a ceiling fan the other day.**
Complete waste of money. He just stands there applauding and saying "Ooh, I love how smooth it is."


**Please describe the attacker…**
Well, 8 letters long, starts with an A!


**I quit my job at the swing factory…**
All day long, it was backward and forward!


**Over Easter the police helicopter was circling our neighbourhood…**
They were looking for some bad eggs!


**I heard Cinderella tried out for the basketball team…**
but she kept running away from the ball!


**Last night I had a dream that I weighed less than a thousandth of a gram…**
I was like, 0mg!

**Two sailors saw an enormous hand come out of the sea. It moves all the way over to one side, then all the way over to the other.**
One sailor says to the other:
"Wow, did you see the size of that wave?"


**I went to the supermarket to get eight cans of Sprite…**
I discovered I'd only picked seven up!


**I hate Russian dolls…**
They're so full of themselves!


**I told my kids if the year 2020 was an Uber…**
I would give it half a star for turning up on time and nothing for instantly catching on fire!


**I read a murder mystery novel about a murder on a rollercoaster…**
So many twists and turns!


**The perfectionist walked into the bar…**
Because it wasn't set high enough!

## TOTALLY AMAZING DAD JOKES

**A friend just asked if I think Advent Calendars will still be around in ten years' time…**
Personally, I think their days are numbered!

**One of my favorite memories as a kid was when my Dad used to put me inside a tire and roll me down a hill…**
They were Goodyears!

**I have a Black Hole joke…**
But it's kind of dark!

**I quit my job as a jockey, I didn't get along with the horse, my boss was shocked….**
she thought our relationship was stable!

**Imagine if Americans switched from pounds to kilograms overnight...**
There would be mass confusion!

**How do you find Will Smith in a snowstorm?**
Look for the fresh prints!

**I went to buy some camouflage pants the other day…**
I couldn't find any!


**I just found out I'm color-blind…**
The diagnosis came completely out of the purple!


**I was born to be a pessimist…**
My blood type is B Negative!


**A neutron walks into a pub and orders a pint.**
The barman says he won't take its money: "No charge."


**Spring is here! I got so excited …**
I wet my plants!


**A man walks into a bar and orders a Corona and 2 Hurricanes Bartender says**
"that will be $20.20"


**Dogs can't operate MRI machines…**
But cats can!

## TOTALLY AMAZING DAD JOKES

**I once bought a dog from a blacksmith.
As soon as I got it home...**
it made a bolt for the door!


**You shouldn't kiss anyone on January 1st because...**
it's only the first date!


**I quit my job as a bouncer...**
I couldn't get my head around the ins and outs!


**5/4 of people admit that they're bad with fractions.**


**Kid:" What's on the TV?"** Dad: "Just some dust."


**I hate jokes about German sausage...**
They're the wurst!


**We are working on a dad joke about hurricanes...**
When we are done you'll be blown away!


**A cheese factory exploded in France.**
Nothing left but Da brie!

**I went to a smoke shop to discover that it has been replaced by an apparel store.**
Clothes, but no cigar!


**I was really angry at my friend Mark for stealing my dictionary. I told him…**
"Mark, my words!"


**For my birthday my children gave me an alarm clock that swore at me instead of buzzing.**
It was quite a rude awakening!

**I have a great joke about nepotism.**
But I'll only tell it to my kids!

# TOTALLY AMAZING DAD JOKES

**I ended up marrying a secret agent,**
she was always sleeping in... she was a sleeper agent!


**Have you heard of the band 1023MB?**
They haven't got a gig yet!


**I wanted to be a doctor…**
but I didn't have the patients!


**Once you have seen one shopping centre...**
You have seen the Mall!


**My 11-year-old grandson has the last name of Mann.**
I really wanted him to have the first name to be whoda. That's right. Whoda Mann!


**Today, my son asked, "Can I have a bookmark?" and I burst into tears.**
11 years old and he still doesn't know my name is Brian!

**If you need help building an ark...**
I Noah guy!


**I'm thinking about getting a new haircut...**
I'm going to mullet over!


**Kid: I'll call you later.**
Dad: Don't call me later, call me Dad.


**I'm so good at sleeping...**
I can do it with my eyes closed!


**I'm sceptical of anyone who tells me they do yoga every day...**
That's a bit of a stretch!


**My friend says to me, "What rhymes with orange?**
And I told him, "No it doesn't!"


**I never buy pre-shredded cheese...**
Because doing it yourself is grate!

## TOTALLY AMAZING DAD JOKES

**I never used to like Dad jokes...**
but they've really groan on me!

**The Invisible Man married the Invisible Woman...**
Their children were nothing to look at!

**Light travels faster than sound...**
This is why some people appear bright until they open their mouths!

**My cat is feeling sick...**
It's not feline well!

**St. Francis worked at Krispy Kreme...**
He was a deep friar!

**The blue whale is so big,
that if you laid it end to end on a basketball court...**
The game would be cancelled!

**I read that by law you must turn on your headlights when it's raining in Sweden…**
but how am I supposed to know when it is raining in Sweden?

**Someone said to me today that they don't understand Cloning…**
I told him, that makes 2 of us!

**I recently got food poisoning from undercooked meat...**
It was fowl!

**I used to hate facial hair…**
But then it grew on me!

**Time flies like an arrow...**
Fruit flies like a banana!

**My dog can do magic tricks...**
He's a Labracadabrador!

# TOTALLY AMAZING DAD JOKES

**Did you hear the one where one statue said to the other statue. "Is that statue?".**
Nah never happened. That's because we had to take them both down.

**Without geometry....**
Life is pointless

**A computer once beat me at chess...**
But it was no match for me at kickboxing!

**I quit my job today as a sign writer...**
I could see the writing on the wall!

**I just quit my job at Starbucks because day after day...**
It was the same old grind!

**My co-worker told a terrible granny smith joke...**
It was appalling!

**A cheeseburger walks into a bar...**
The bartender says, "sorry sir we don't serve food here".

**Kid:" How is that water?"**
Dad: "Wet."


**I was addicted to the hokey pokey…**
But thankfully, I turned myself around!


**Two men walk into a bar…**
You'd think one of them would have seen it!


**I complained about a place selling fireplaces the other day due to false advertising…**
They said they were having a fire sale!


**I had a Girlfriend who was into soccer…**
She was a keeper!


**A man was recently hospitalised with 6 plastic horses inside of him…**
The doctor is describing his condition as stable!


**Life's like a bird…**
It's pretty cute until it poops on your head!

## TOTALLY AMAZING DAD JOKES

**I used to operate the kiln in a pottery factory...**
Then I got fired!


**I just had double knee surgery in Japan..**
I now have Japa-knees!


**I once had a dream I was floating in an ocean of orange soda...**
It was more of a fanta sea!


**I just went to an emotional wedding...**
Even the cake was in tiers!


**I had a job fixing laptops...**
The job was easy, very open and shut!


**The first time I used an elevator...**
It was very uplifting and then it let me down!


**"Dad, please make me a sandwich."**
"Poof! You're a sandwich!"

**I just flew in from New York...**
And boy are my arms tired!.


**I missed out on a promotion at the ladder factory...**
They said it was beyond my reach!


**If you want a job in the moisturizer industry...**
The best advice I can give is...to apply daily!


**Two soldiers are in a tank...**
One looks to the other and says, "glub glub glub glub glub."


**Two goldfish are in a tank,
one turns to the other and says...**
How do we drive this thing?


**There are three types of people...**
Those who can count, and those who can't!


**I've had amnesia for as long as I can...**

## TOTALLY AMAZING DAD JOKES

**I accidentally handed my wife the superglue instead of her lipstick...**
She still isn't talking to me!


**What do you call a donkey with only three legs?**
A wonkey!


**I went to the corner shop today...**
Bought four corners!


**Money can't buy you happiness?**
Well, check this out, I bought myself a Happy Meal!


**What rhymes with boo and stinks?**
You!


**Would a cardboard belt be a waist of paper?**


**My boss told me to have a good day...**
So, I went home!

**I used to tune tv's for a living…**
My parents were ecstatic!


**I'm arguing with my insurance company…**
The roof blew off my house… they say I'm not covered


**The circle is the most ridiculous shape in the world…**
There's absolutely no point to it!


**A red ship collided with a blue ship…**
All the sailors were marooned!


**I don't have a beer gut…**
I have a protective covering for my rock hard abs!


**Last night I dreamed I was muffler…**
I woke up exhausted!


**A new shop has opened called Moderation…**
They have everything in there!

## TOTALLY AMAZING DAD JOKES

**I told my mom I was going to make a car out of spaghetti...**
you should have seen her face when I drove straight pasta!


**If a stitch in time saves nine...**
Imagine how much a sewing machine will save!


**I paid a guy to help blow up some balloons...**
I had to fire him, he sucked!.


**Don't spell part backward...**
It's a trap!


**I took the shell off my racing snail thinking it would make him go faster...**
But instead now he's more sluggish!

**Do you think duck tape is made out of....**
Real ducks?


**I just watched a program about beavers...**
It was the best dam program I've ever seen!


**I wanted some Helicopter flavoured potato chips…**
But they only had Plane!


**My uncle named his dogs Rolex and Timex...**
They're his watch dogs!


**I gave all my dead batteries away today...**
Free of charge!


**Do you know the last thing my grandfather said to me before he kicked the bucket?**
"Grandson, watch how far I can kick this bucket."


**I made a Dad joke and I am not a Dad…**
Does that make me a faux pa?

## TOTALLY AMAZING DAD JOKES

**A recent study has shown that women who carry a little extra weight live longer...**
Than the men who mention it!

**My hotel tried to charge me ten dollars extra for air conditioning...**
That wasn't cool at all!.

**I don't trust stairs...**
They're always up to something!

**When my wife told me to stop impersonating a flamingo...**
I had to put my foot down!

**A locksmith had to go to court to give evidence last week...**
Apparently, he was the key witness!

**I've been bored recently so I've decided to take up fencing.**
The neighbors said they will call the police unless I put it back!

**I quit my job as a forestry worker and started my own business…**
It was time to branch out!


**You can buy a new type of broom from Amazon…**
It's doing so well, that Its sweeping the nation!


**Someone complimented my parking today! They left a sweet note on my windshield that said…**
"parking fine."


**I will always love my kids unconditionally…**
As long as they meet my conditions!


**I remember a cow my neighbor had named Winnie…**
Because Winnie poo's!


**I pretended to be a superhero while riding a horse bareback…**
I was Thor for days afterwards!

# TOTALLY AMAZING DAD JOKES

**I like telling Dad jokes...**
Sometimes he laughs!


**I fired my builder...**
He wasn't really nailing it!


**I started a business collecting old penny's...**
It didn't make cents!


**A positive attitude may not solve all your problems...**
But it will annoy enough people to make it worth the effort!


**Velcro is the ultimate rip-off.**


**I once got fired from a canned juice factory...**
Apparently, I couldn't concentrate!


**Cosmetic surgery used to be such a taboo subject...**
Now you can talk about Botox and nobody raises an eyebrow!

**I thought about going on an all-macadamia diet…**
But that's just nuts!


**I have a vacuum cleaner joke…**
But it really sucks!


**I tried scaring the tallest man alive yesterday…**
His head hit the ceiling!


**I got all my looks from my father…**
Mostly just the look of disappointment!


**I think my wife is putting glue on my antique weapons collection…**
She denies it but I'm sticking to my guns!


**If you thought 2020 was bad, then 2022 is going to be horrible…**
Because 2022 is 2020, too!


**If two vegans are having an argument…**
Is it still considered a beef?

# TOTALLY AMAZING DAD JOKES

**Kid: "Shall I put the TV on?"**
Dad: "You think it will suit you?"

**I keep having a nightmare where I'm a marquee, then one where I'm a tepee...**
The doctor says I'm too tense!

**I swallowed some food coloring...**
My Doctor said I might feel blue for a few days!

**I recently got locked out of a piano shop...**
I couldn't fine the keys!

**I have a few jokes about unemployed people…**
But none of them work!


**How do you make holy water?**
You boil the hell out of it!

**I tried to make a chemistry joke…**
But got no reaction!

**The Chemistry joke was sodium funny…**
I slapped my neon that one!

**England doesn't have a kidney bank…**
But it does have a Liverpool!

**Let me tell you about my grandfather. He was a good man, a brave man. He had the heart of a lion…**
And a lifetime ban from the zoo!

**What washes up on tiny beaches?**
Microwaves

## TOTALLY AMAZING DAD JOKES

**My Sister tried to apply for a job at the post office, but they wouldn't letter...**
They said only mails work here!

**I named my Wi-Fi Modem 'The Titanic', so when people try to connect...**
It says, "The Titanic is syncing."

**My ex-wife still misses me...**
But her aim is starting to improve!

**During World War 2, the man who survived pepper spray and mustard gas became...**
A seasoned veteran!

**When I was younger, I had a photographic memory...**
But I never developed it!

**When everything is coming your way...**
You're in the wrong lane!

**What are the strongest days of the week?**
Saturday and Sunday, the rest are weekdays!


**I lost my job at the bank after a woman asked me to check her balance…**
So, I pushed her over!


**Jim broke his finger today…**
But on the other hand, he was completely fine!


**Being a superhero that had the ability to fly would be so…** uplifting


**What do you call the ghost of a chicken?**
A poultry-geist!


**Why are frogs so happy?**
They eat whatever bugs them!


**The cross-eyed teacher…**
Couldn't control his pupils!

## TOTALLY AMAZING DAD JOKES

**When life gives you melons...**
You're dyslexic!

**Whether glass coffins will become successful...**
Remains to be seen!

**All chemistry School Teachers know...**
That alcohol is always a solution!

**This guy I knew collected candy canes...**
They were all in mint condition!

**What do you call a bee that can't make up its mind?**
Maybe

**Never discuss infinity with a mathematician...**
They can go on about it forever!

**My Neighbor just knocked on my door and told me my dogs are chasing people on bikes...**
That's ridiculous. My dogs don't even own bikes!

**What do you call the girlfriend of a hippie?**
Mississippi!


**"I have a split personality,"** said Tom, being frank.


**Did you hear about the guy whose whole left side was cut off...**
He's all right now!


**If a child refuses to take a nap...**
Is he resisting a rest?


**In America, using the metric system can get you in legal trouble. In fact, if you sneer at any other method of measuring liquids...**
You may be held in contempt of quart!


**I was part of a union at the peanut butter factory...**
They were all nuts!


**I can't own an electric car...**
I'm too negative!

# TOTALLY AMAZING DAD JOKES

**I can always tell if someone is lying just by looking at them…**
I can also tell if they are standing.


**My greatest achievement is raising my kids on a trampoline...**
They're my offspring!


**I ordered a chicken and an egg online...**
I'll let you know!


**Two cats swam the English Channel. They were called One Two Three and Un Deux Trois. Which cat won?**
One Two Three, because Un Deux Trois cat sank.


**I was playing chess with my friend and he said, "Let's make this interesting."**
So, we stopped playing chess.


**I'll call you later...**
Don't call me later, call me Dad!

**I was fired from the laundromat due to a complaint...**
I was hung out to dry!


**I can rely on my fingers...**
I can count on all of them!


**Dad, can you put my shoes on..**
No, I don't think they'll fit me!


**I once ate a dictionary…**
It gave me thesaurus throat I've ever had!


**For years I thought every taxi driver's name was....**
Roger over and out!


**I only know 25 letters of the alphabet...**
I don't know Y!


**What do you call a cow who is good at yoga?**
A liar

## TOTALLY AMAZING DAD JOKES

**A cow just quit her job...**
Too many meatings!

**I tried to catch the fog...**
I mist!

**What do you call a goat drunk on eggnog...**
Mehrrrry!

**An apple pie in Jamaica is $1.50, a cherry pie in Barbados is $1.60 and a mince pie in Trinidad is $1.80...**
These are the pie rates of the Caribbean!

HETA DAWSON   CORIN HEALY

# Punny Dad Jokes

*The Punniest of all Jokes*

## TOTALLY AMAZING DAD JOKES

**What do you call a laughing motorcycle?**
A Yamahahaha.


**Did you hear about the 2 silk worms in a race?**
It ended in a tie!


**I hate how funerals are always at 9 a.m.**
I'm not really a mourning person.


**Did you hear about the man who was accidentally buried alive?**
It was a grave mistake.


**I'm a big fan of whiteboards.**
I find them quite re-markable.


**When she saw her first strands of grey hair…**
She thought she'd dye!


**Q. How much money does a pirate pay for corn?**
A. A buccaneer.

**I had to clean out my spice rack and found everything was too old and had to be thrown out.**
What a waste of thyme.

**I saw an ad for burial plots, and thought to myself…**
This is the last thing I need!

**Q. Why was King Arthur's army too tired to fight?**
A. It had too many sleepless knights.

## TOTALLY AMAZING DAD JOKES

**Yesterday, a clown held the door open for me...**
It was such a nice jester!


**Did you hear about the auto body shop that just opened?**
It comes highly wreck-a-mended!


**Atoms are untrustworthy little critters...**
They make up everything!


**So, what if I can't spell Armageddon?**
It's not the end of the world!


**I put all my spare cash into an origami business...**
It folded!


**I wrote a song about a tortilla...**
Well it's more of a wrap!

**What did the dog say when he sat on sandpaper?**
Ruff!

**I bought some cool shoes from a drug dealer...**
I don't know what he laced them with, but I've been tripping all day!


**I wanted to learn how to drive a stick shift...**
But I couldn't find the manual!


**I wasn't originally going to get a brain transplant...**
But then I changed my mind!


**My friend entered a pun contest. He entered ten, figuring at least one of them would win...**
But no pun in ten did!

## TOTALLY AMAZING DAD JOKES

**Acupuncture is a jab well done.**

**What do you do if your dog chews a dictionary?**
Take the words out of his mouth!

**Someone stole my toilet...**
I called the Police but they had nothing to go on!

**Q. Did you hear about the man who fell into an upholstery machine?**
A. He's fully recovered.

**Don't interrupt someone working intently on a puzzle. Chances are...**
You'll hear some crosswords!

**One bird can't make a pun...**
But toucan!

**Why should you never fart on an elevator?**
It's wrong on so many levels!

**What does C.S. Lewis keep at the back of his wardrobe?**
Narnia business!


**A man sued an airline company after it lost his luggage…**
Sadly, he lost his case!


**I was going to make myself a belt made from watches…**
But then I realized it would be a waist of time!


**The past, the present, and the future walk into a bar…**
It was tense!


**6:30 is the best time on a clock…**
Hands down!


**I asked my French friend if she likes to play video games…**
She said, "Wii."

## TOTALLY AMAZING DAD JOKES

**What did the librarian say when the books were in a mess?**
We ought to be ashamed of ourshelves!

**The machine at the coin factory just suddenly stopped working, with no explanation...**
It doesn't make any cents!

**I want to be cremated...**
My whole life I wanted a smoking hot body!

**Who was Socrates' worst student?**
Mediocrities!

**Who was his busiest student?**
The one with a lot on his Plato!

**Q. What sound does a sleeping T-Rex make?**
A. A dino-snore.

**What do you get if you cross a chicken and a cow?**
A roost beef!

**My ex used to hit me with stringed instruments…**
If only I had known about her history of violins!

**Why did Adele go to a fortune teller?**
To say hello from the other side!

**My wife said to me that she saw Moose falling from the sky…**
I said to her, "it's reindeer."

**Geology rocks…**
But Geography is where it's at!

## TOTALLY AMAZING DAD JOKES

**Small babies get be delivered by a stork...**
But the heavier ones need a crane!

**I lost my mood ring...**
I can't work out how to feel about it!

**My brother drove his new car into a tree...**
He found out how his Mercedes bends!

**Some animals at the zoo escaped from the Aquatic department...**
It was otter chaos!

**Long fairy tales...**
Tend to dragon!

**Q. What's the difference between a hippo and a Zippo?**
A. A hippo is really heavy, and a Zippo
B. is a little lighter.

**I made a pun about the wind**
But it blows!

**I went to a seafood disco last week...**
And pulled a mussel!


**My friend is obsessed with
bird watching at night…**
He's an owlcoholic!

TOTALLY AMAZING DAD JOKES

# Down Under Dad Jokes
*Dad Jokes from the lands Downunder*

**What do you call an owl with one leg longer than the other?**
Not even owl.


**What do you call a bull with no legs?**
A ranch slider.


**What did the statue say the other statue?**
Statue bro?

**Statue to the cat: statue bro?**
Cat: Nah, it's me auw

TOTALLY AMAZING DAD JOKES

**What do you call a Frenchman wearing Jandals?**
Phillipe Phillop.


**Me: I saw a kiwi…**
Dad: "Must have been busting!"


**Why did the cockatoo sit on the clock?**
So he'd be on time!

**What Australian animal can jump higher than the Sydney Harbour Bridge?**
All of them – because bridges can't jump!

**Did you know you can't "run" thru' a campground?**
You can only "ran". 'Coz it is past tents!


**The shortest sentence is "I am.",
What is the longest sentence?**
"I Do"


**What do you call a kangaroo that is a dead set genius?**
A quantum leap!

**Two Aussies are drinking together. One says, "When I die, will you promise to pour a beer on my grave?"**
The other replies, "No worries mate,
but I'll have to pass it through my kidneys first."

## TOTALLY AMAZING DAD JOKES

**When is a bear not a bear?**
When he doesn't have the right koalifications!


**Why did the wombat decide to cross over the road?**
To see his flatmate!


**How do you say sorry to a koala bear?**
Ensure that you BEAR your heart and soul with feeling!


**I met a bloke from Australia who worked in Information Technology. I asked him…**
"Do you come from a LAN down under?"


**Did you hear about the two baked beans that hitchhiked around Australia?**
They ended up in Cairns!


**What did the Aussie fella do after he finished raking the leaves?**
He fell outta the tree!

**What's the difference between the Aussie Rugby team and the Sydney harbour Bridge?**
Not everyone has walked over the Sydney harbour bridge!

**Why aren't the Wallabies Rugby team members allowed to own a dog?**
Because they can't hold on to a lead.

**What do you call an Aussie that scores well on an IQ test?**
A cheat!

**What do you get when you cross breed a kangaroo with a donkey?**
A kick ass!

**What do ya call a lazy baby kangaroo?**
A pouch potato!

**Why do mummy kangaroos always hate wet days?**
Because their kids play inside!

## TOTALLY AMAZING DAD JOKES

**What is a kangaroo's favourite kind of music genre?**
Hip Hop!

**Did you hear about the amazing mountain ranges in Southern NZ?**
They are Remarkable!

**What's the difference between a smart Kiwi and a unicorn?**
Nothing, they're both fictional characters!

**Did you hear about the winner of the New Zealand beauty contest?**
Me neither!

**How do Kiwi's find sheep in long grass?**
Delightful!

**I think my wife has started to show the first signs of Alzheimers...**
She said she can't remember what she ever saw in me!

**How do Aussies start every joke?**
By looking over their shoulder!


**What do you call a kiwi with 100 girlfriends?**
A sheep farmer!


**What do you call a Kiwi in the knockout stages of the Soccer World Cup?**
A Referee.


**What do you call an Australian who is always late?**
Late, Mate!


**Chris Hemsworth is Australian and Thor is from space...**
Does that make him an Australien?


**Do you know why I quit my job at a Test Cricket umpire?**
It was the same thing over and over


**When you think about it,**
technically all Australian submarines are down under

## TOTALLY AMAZING DAD JOKES

**What do you call a Boomerang that does not come back?**
A Stick

**What is the difference between yoghurt and Australia?**
Yoghurt has some culture!

**What's the difference between an Australian or New Zealander visiting the USof A and a Canoe?**
A canoe tips!

**A British man is visiting Australia. The customs agent asks him, "Do you have a criminal record?"**
The British man replies, "I didn't think you needed one to get into Australia anymore."

**How many Aussies does it take to screw in a lightbulb?**
Three. One to hold the bulb, and two to turn the ladder.

**What martial art did the Ozzie Farmer learn?**
Fencing

**An Aussie said, "Take away your snow capped mountains, culture, and good food, and what would New Zealand be?"**
The kiwi answered, "Australia".

**Why was the farmer upset?**
Baaaaabra left him

**Why did the farmer send his eggs back?**
They were poached

**I forgot how to throw a boomerang the other day**
then it came back to me.

# Conclusion

Our mission at Konnectd Kids is to ensure you and your family have fun and that with the help of our books that you turn these fun experiences into remarkable memories!

Comedians Heta Dawson and Corin Healy have worked to create and collate a collection of jokes that we hoped you thoroughly enjoyed. Our *Totally Amazing Dad Jok*es' book was made specifically to share the fun and the humor from great, good, and terrible Dad jokes

Thank you for the interest in this book and we invite you to take a look at our Konnectd Kids Publishing catalogue for any other books that may be of interest.

HETA DAWSON   CORIN HEALY

**Visit us at:**
www.konnectdkids.com

**Our Books and Products:**
www.konnectdkids.com/books
www.konnectdsupply.com
www.etsy.com/shop/konnectd
konnectd.redbubble.com

**Find and tag us on Instagram**
@Konnectdkids or #konnectdkids

**Follow us on Facebook**
facebook.com/konnectdkids

**Join our Facebook Group
(Free Books and giveaways)**
https://www.facebook.com/groups/konnectdkidsgroup

www.ingramcontent.com/pod-product-compliance
Lightning Source LLC
Chambersburg PA
CBHW051402290426
44108CB00015B/2116